Essential COOKING SERIES

COMPREHENSIVE, STEP BY STEP COOKING

Home
Baking

BUDGET BOOKS

Food Editor: Neil Hargreaves
Cover Design: Budget Books
Prepress: Graphic Print Group

 Essential Cooking Series: Home Baking
First published in 2008 by Budget Books Pty Ltd
45–55 Fairchild Street
Heatherton, Victoria, 3202, Australia

10 9 8 7 6 5 4
13 12 11 10 09

Disclaimer: The nutritional information listed under each recipe does not
include the nutrient content of garnishes or any accompaniments not listed
in specific quantitites in the ingredient list. The nutritional information for
each recipe is an estimate only, and may vary depending on the brand of
ingredients used, and due to natural biological variations in the composition
of natural foods such as meat, fish, fruit and vegetables. The nutritional
information was calculated by using Foodworks dietary analysis software
(Version 3, Xyris Software Pty Ltd, Highgate Hill, Queensland, Australia) based
on the Australian food composition tables and food manufacturers' data.
Where not specified, ingredients are always analysed as average or medium,
not small or large.

ISBN: 978 1 7418 1468 2

Printed and bound in China

Contents

An introduction to home baking

The aroma of a freshly baked cake, the taste of a still-warm biscuit, the fascination of watching bread dough rise, the flavour of homemade pastry and the compliments of family and friends is what baking is all about. With today's busy lifestyle, many people think of cakes and cookies as something that mum or grandma used to make, but which now come from the supermarket. Baking is one of the most satisfying and economical forms of home cooking. If you have hungry teenagers to feed, a packet of biscuits can be gone in five minutes, whereas a batch of 50 or more biscuits can be made for a fraction of the cost and will last at least twice as long! In this book you will find recipes not only for old favourites such as sticky date pudding, apple pie and potato and cheese pie, but also for those new ones like chocolate-mocha cake, prune and orange muffins and peach and hazelnut crumble.

NOTE TO READERS

For consistent results when cooking, and especially when baking, it is important to weigh and measure ingredients accurately. All spoon and cup measures given in this book are level; flour is white plain flour and sugar is white unless otherwise stated. The sizes of cans vary between countries and manufacturers: you may find the quantities in this book are slightly different from what is available. Use the can size nearest to the suggested size in the recipe.

Many cake recipes begin with the creaming of the butter and sugar. This is an important process, as little bubbles of air are trapped in the mixture and it is this air which helps to produce a light-textured cake. The butter should be softened for the creaming process and the mixture beaten until it is creamy and fluffy and almost doubled in volume. Creaming can be done with a balloon whisk, wooden spoon, electric mixer or food processor. After the creaming process, an egg or eggs are often added to the mixture. The egg white forms a layer around each bubble of air and as the cake cooks, the egg white coagulates and forms a wall around each bubble, preventing the bubbles from bursting and so ruining the cake. As the cake cooks, the air bubbles expand and the cake rises.

Do not open the oven door while baking until at least halfway through the recommended cooking time, or anything relying on rising can be affected. With the sudden drop in temperature, baking stops expanding and muffins and cakes can sink. The oven should be preheated to the correct temperature before baking. If you're baking more than one item, arrange the pans and trays so that they do not touch each other or the sides of the oven. It's important to fill the cake pans and muffin tins correctly to ensure a successful result. If your batter is soft it can be poured into the cake pan; however, a firm batter should be spooned in and spread out

evenly. For light batters, only fill the pan half to two-thirds full; heavy batters can fill as much as three-quarters of the pan.

IS THE BAKING FINISHED?

Test your bake just before the end of the cooking. For most baking, insert a skewer into the thickest part of your food. In the case of cakes, if it comes away clean, your cake is cooked. Alternatively, you can gently press the top of a cake with your fingertips. When cooked, the depression will spring back quickly. When the cake starts to leave the sides of the pan it's another indication that a cake is cooked. If it is a savoury strudel, test for how firm the filling feels: if it's soft inside it is a good indication that your dish is complete and ready to remove from the oven.

COOLING A CAKE

You will find that a freshly baked cake is very fragile. Allow a cake to stand for a short time in the pan before turning onto a wire rack to cool. Before turning out a cake, loosen the sides with a spatula or palette knife. Turn the cake onto a wire rack, then immediately invert onto a second wire rack so that the top of the cake is not marked with indentations from the rack. If you do not have a second wire rack, invert the cake onto a clean cloth on your hand then turn it onto the wire rack.

STORING BAKED GOODS

Allow cakes to cool completely before placing them in an airtight container, or condensation will accumulate in the container and cause the cake to go mouldy. Keeping times for cakes vary depending on the ingredients used. A fatless sponge will only stay fresh for 1 to 2 days, while one made with fat will keep fresh for 3 days. Cakes made using the creaming method usually keep fresh for up to a week. Light fruit cakes keep for 2 to 3 weeks and heavy rich fruit cakes will store for a month or more.

Most baked goods can be frozen successfully. Wrap them in freezer wrap or place in a freezer bag and seal. If freezing several items, wrap each separately or place freezer wrap or waxed paper between them so that they are easy to remove. To thaw a frozen cake, leave in the wrapping and thaw at room temperature. Large cakes will take 3 to 4 hours to thaw, layer cakes 1 to 2 hours and small cakes about 30 minutes. Pies and tarts also thaw according to size.

PREPARING A CAKE PAN OR TIN

You need to grease and flour a cake pan. Using a pastry brush, lightly brush the pan with melted butter or margarine, then sprinkle with flour and shake to coat evenly. Invert pan on a work surface and tap gently to remove excess flour. To grease and line a round cake pan, place cake pan on a large piece of greaseproof paper and trace around the base using a pencil, then cut out the shape. Grease pan and line with paper. A deep cake pan should be lined on the bottom and sides. Use a double-folded strip of greaseproof paper 6 cm higher than the cake pan and long enough to fit around

the pan and to overlap by about 2.5 cm. On the folded edge, turn up about 2.5 cm and crease, then, using scissors, snip at regular intervals across the margin as far as the fold. Cut out a piece of greaseproof paper to line the bottom of the pan, as described previously. Grease the pan and place the strip around the sides of the pan with the snipped margin lying flat on the bottom of the pan. Ensure that the ends overlap, so that the sides are completely covered by the paper. Place the bottom piece of greaseproof paper in the pan to cover the snipped margin.

To line a loaf pan, cut a strip of greaseproof paper the width of the bottom of the pan and long enough to come up the shorter sides of the pan and overlap by 2.5 cm. Grease the pan and line with the paper. When the cake is cooked, the unlined sides can be loosened with a knife and the paper ends can be used to lift out the cake.

Pastries and strudels are best baked on a sheet of greaseproof paper, making them less likely to stick and also making it easier to move them to a cooling rack after baking.

Following the tips above will have you baking with ease and on your way to being a confident and sought-after baker within your group of friends! Sometimes the old-fashioned skills are the most rewarding.

Enjoy.

Lemon-scented fish pie

INGREDIENTS

1 kg potatoes, cut into even-sized
  pieces
55 g butter
1 onion, chopped
2 stalks celery, sliced
2 tablespoons plain flour
1 cup fish stock
finely grated zest and juice of
  1 large lemon
salt and freshly ground black pepper
455 g cod loin, cut into cubes
170 g mussels, cooked until shells
  open and shelled
2 tablespoons fresh parsley, chopped
4 tablespoons milk
serves 4

PREPARATION TIME
20 minutes

COOKING TIME
1 hour

1 Preheat the oven to 220°C. Cook the potatoes in boiling salted water for
15–20 minutes until tender, then drain.

2 Meanwhile, melt half the butter in a large saucepan, add the onion
and celery and cook for 2–3 minutes, until softened. Add the flour and
cook, stirring, for 1 minute. Slowly add the stock and cook, stirring, until
thickened. Add the lemon zest and juice and season with salt and pepper.

3 Remove the sauce from the heat, stir in the cod, mussels and parsley, then
transfer to an ovenproof dish.

4 Mash the potatoes with the remaining butter and the milk. Season, then
spread the potato evenly over the fish with a fork. Bake for 30–40 minutes,
until the sauce is bubbling and the topping starts to brown.

NUTRITIONAL VALUE PER SERVE	FAT 14.5 G	CARBOHYDRATE 44 G	PROTEIN 36.5 G

Clapshot pie

INGREDIENTS

1 tablespoon olive or sunflower oil
1 small onion, chopped
1 small carrot, finely chopped
40 g bacon, chopped
600 g minced beef
1 cup beef stock
2 tablespoons tomato sauce
1 tablespoon Worcestershire sauce
1 teaspoon fresh thyme, chopped
salt and freshly ground black pepper
2 tablespoons chopped fresh parsley,
   plus extra to garnish
topping
350 g potatoes, chopped
350 g swede, chopped
40 g butter
120 ml light cream
salt and freshly ground black pepper
nutmeg, freshly grated
serves 4

1 Preheat the oven to 200°C. Heat the oil in a frying pan, then fry the onion, carrot and bacon for 10 minutes or until browned. Add the beef and fry for 10–15 minutes. Spoon off any fat, then stir in the stock, sauces, thyme and seasoning. Simmer, partly covered, for 45 minutes, stirring occasionally, until thickened. Add a little water if the mixture becomes too dry.

2 Meanwhile, cook the potatoes and swede in boiling salted water for 15–20 minutes, until tender. Drain, then mash with half the butter and the cream. Season with salt, pepper and nutmeg.

3 Transfer the beef to a 1½ litre shallow ovenproof dish, then stir in the parsley. Smooth over the potato and swede mixture, then fluff it up with a fork and dot with the remaining butter. Bake for 35–45 minutes, until browned. Garnish with parsley.

PREPARATION TIME
20 minutes

COOKING TIME
1 hour 55 minutes

NUTRITIONAL VALUE PER SERVE	FAT 28 G	CARBOHYDRATE 19.5 G	PROTEIN 29 G

Italian spinach tart

INGREDIENTS

pastry
2 cups plain flour
pinch salt
125 g sweet butter
¹/₃ cup iced water
filling
500 g spinach
200 g fresh ricotta cheese
4 eggs, beaten
60 g parmesan cheese, grated
nutmeg, grated
salt and freshly ground black pepper
serves 4

PREPARATION TIME
20 minutes, plus 30 minutes refrigeration

COOKING TIME
1 hour

1 Preheat oven to 200°C. Sift the flour and salt into a large bowl. Cut the butter into small pieces, adding it to the flour. Rub in the butter until the mixture resembles breadcrumbs. Don't overdo this, as the butter will be blended more thoroughly later.

2 Make a well in the centre of the mixture. Mix in the iced water and combine quickly with a knife. Press the dough together with your fingers.

3 Turn out on to a floured board and knead lightly until smooth. Roll into a ball. Brush off excess flour. Wrap in greaseproof paper and refrigerate for 20–30 minutes before using.

4 Roll out the pastry and use it to line a 25 cm flan ring. Trim the edges. Prick the base lightly with a fork and line with baking paper. Half-fill with dried beans and bake blind (see glossary, page 58) in a preheated hot oven for 7 minutes. Remove the beans and bake for a further 5 minutes.

5 Meanwhile, wash the spinach and place it in a saucepan with the water clinging to the leaves. Cook, covered, until tender. Then drain, squeeze dry, let cool and chop finely. In a bowl, beat the ricotta until smooth, then beat in the eggs, parmesan, nutmeg and spinach. Season the mixture with salt and pepper and pour it into the prebaked pastry shell. Bake at 180°C for 25–30 minutes until golden and set. Serve cold.

NUTRITIONAL VALUE PER SERVE	FAT 43.5 G	CARBOHYDRATE 52 G	PROTEIN 29 G

Wax-bean tart with caramelised onions

INGREDIENTS

200 g puff pastry, defrosted if frozen
butter for greasing
1 tablespoon olive oil
2 onions, sliced
1 teaspoon salt
$\frac{1}{2}$ teaspoon caster sugar
400 g canned wax beans, drained
2 tablespoons parmesan cheese,
　freshly grated
2 tablespoons gruyère cheese,
　freshly grated
1 teaspoon white pepper
3 small eggs, beaten
5 spring onions, finely chopped
100 g crème fraîche
serves 4

PREPARATION TIME
30 minutes, plus
10 minutes chilling
and 10 minutes
cooling

COOKING TIME
1 hour

1 Preheat the oven to 220°C. Roll out the pastry on a lightly
floured surface and use it to line a greased 20 cm round tart tin.
Refrigerate for 10 minutes.

2 Heat the oil in a heavy-based saucepan, add the onions, half of the
salt and sugar and cook over a low heat for 25 minutes or until the
onions have caramelised and turned golden. Set aside.

3 Purée the wax beans in a food processor or with a hand blender,
or mash with a fork. Transfer to a bowl and stir in the parmesan,
gruyère, pepper, eggs and remaining salt. Mix thoroughly, then
pour into the pastry case. Bake for 30–35 minutes, until the top
has risen and is golden. Leave to cool for 10 minutes. Meanwhile,
mix together the spring onions and crème fraîche. Spoon over the
tart, top with the caramelised onions and serve.

NUTRITIONAL VALUE PER SERVE	FAT **28** G	CARBOHYDRATE **21** G	PROTEIN **10** G

Capsicum and onion tart

INGREDIENTS

40 ml chicken stock
2 teaspoons brown sugar
2 onions, thinly sliced
8 sheets filo pastry
50 ml water
1 tablespoon oil
180 g ricotta cheese, drained
2 tablespoons fresh basil, chopped
freshly ground black pepper
1 small red and 1 small green
   capsicum, roasted and cut into
   thin strips

serves 4

1 Preheat the oven to 175°C. Place stock and brown sugar in a nonstick frying pan and cook over a medium heat for 3–4 minutes or until sugar dissolves. Add onions and cook, stirring, for 15 minutes or until onions start to caramelise.

2 Layer the pastry sheets, brushing between each layer with water. Brush the top sheet of pastry with oil and use layered pastry to line a lightly greased 18 x 28 cm shallow cake tin. Roll pastry edges to neaten.

3 Place ricotta cheese, basil and black pepper to taste in a bowl and mix together. Spread ricotta mixture over pastry, then top with onions and roasted capsicums and bake for 20 minutes or until pastry is crisp and golden.

PREPARATION TIME
15 minutes

COOKING TIME
45 minutes

NUTRITIONAL VALUE PER SERVE	FAT 7.5 G	CARBOHYDRATE 15 G	PROTEIN 6.5 G

Spinach and roquefort tart

INGREDIENTS

300 g unsweetened pastry, thawed
  if frozen
200 g fresh spinach, thick stalks
  discarded
freshly ground black pepper
pinch of nutmeg, freshly grated
100 g roquefort or other blue
  cheese, cubed
1 small egg, beaten
285 ml light cream

serves 4

1 Preheat the oven to 200°C. Roll out the pastry on a lightly floured surface and use it to line a 20 cm flan dish. Prick the pastry base with a fork and bake blind (see glossary, page 58) for 10 minutes or until lightly golden.

2 Meanwhile, rinse the spinach and place it in a saucepan with the water clinging to its leaves. Cook, covered, for 3–4 minutes until wilted. Drain, leave to cool slightly, then squeeze out the excess water. Spoon the spinach into the pastry base and spread with the back of a wooden spoon. Season with pepper and nutmeg, then add the cheese. Mix together the egg and cream and pour over the top.

3 Bake for 30 minutes or until the filling has risen and is golden. Leave to rest for 10 minutes before serving in slices.

PREPARATION TIME
20 minutes, plus
10 minutes standing

COOKING TIME
45 minutes

NUTRITIONAL VALUE PER SERVE	FAT **37.5** G	CARBOHYDRATE **29** G	PROTEIN **11.5** G

Potato, cheese and onion pie

INGREDIENTS

455 g fresh shortcrust pastry
455 g waxy potatoes, very thinly
  sliced
1 small onion, very thinly sliced
100 g red leicester (or hard cheese),
  finely grated
salt and freshly ground black pepper
145 ml cream
serves 4

PREPARATION TIME
30 minutes, plus
10 minutes cooling

COOKING TIME
1 hour 15 minutes

1 Preheat the oven to 180°C. Roll two-thirds of the pastry on to a
lightly floured work surface and use it to line a 23 cm flan dish.
Arrange the potatoes in a single layer over the base of the dish,
then top with a layer each of the onion and cheese. Repeat until
the potatoes are all used, seasoning well between each layer.
Pour over the cream.

2 Roll out the remaining pastry to make a lid. Lightly dampen
the edges of the pie with water. Place the pastry lid on top and
pinch the edges together to seal well.

3 Bake for 1–1¼ hours, until the potatoes and onions are tender.
Leave for 10 minutes before serving to allow the cheese to
cool slightly.

NUTRITIONAL VALUE PER SERVE   FAT 53 G   CARBOHYDRATE 63 G   PROTEIN 16.5 G

Quince paste, blue cheese and walnut fingers

INGREDIENTS

2 cups plain flour
4 teaspoons baking powder
2 tablespoons sugar
2 eggs
2 tablespoons olive oil
1 cup milk
120 g quince paste
140 g blue cheese
26 walnut pieces
makes about 12 fingers

PREPARATION TIME
10 minutes

COOKING TIME
20 minutes

1 Preheat the oven to 180°C. Sift flour and baking powder into a bowl. Mix in sugar. Make a well in the centre of the dry ingredients.

2 Lightly beat the eggs and oil together to combine. Add milk and pour egg mixture into dry ingredients. Mix quickly to just combine.

3 Line the base of a 20 x 30 cm sponge roll tin with baking paper. Pour mixture into the tin.

4 Slice quince paste finely. Arrange paste in rows about 1.5 cm apart over mixture. Crumble over blue cheese and put a walnut piece on each quince paste slice.

5 Bake for 15–20 minutes or until mixture springs back when lightly touched. Serve cut into fingers.

NUTRITIONAL VALUE PER SERVE	FAT **13** G	CARBOHYDRATE **23** G	PROTEIN **7.5** G

Spinach and ricotta bake

INGREDIENTS

1 tablespoon olive oil
1 medium onion, chopped
500 g frozen spinach, defrosted
150 g ricotta
50 g pine nuts
$1/8$ teaspoon ground nutmeg
salt and freshly ground black pepper
6 sheets filo pastry
1–2 tablespoons olive oil for brushing
1 beaten egg for glazing
serves 4

PREPARATION TIME
15 minutes

COOKING TIME
30 minutes

1 Preheat the oven to 200°C. Heat the oil in a heavy-based frying pan, add the onion and fry for 3–4 minutes, until slightly softened.

2 Put the spinach into a colander, press to squeeze out any excess water, then roughly chop. Place in a bowl and add the onion, ricotta, pine nuts and nutmeg. Season with salt and plenty of pepper and mix well.

3 Lightly oil a 20 x 20 cm ovenproof dish. Add the spinach mixture, pressing down gently to form an even layer. Place a sheet of filo on top, folding it to fit the tin, then lightly brush with oil. Repeat with the remaining filo, brushing each sheet with oil before placing the next on top.

4 Mark the top into 4 portions using a sharp knife, then brush with the egg. Cook for 25 minutes or until golden brown. Cut into portions and serve.

NUTRITIONAL VALUE PER SERVE	FAT 24 G	CARBOHYDRATE 11 G	PROTEIN 14 G

Mushroom and feta strudel

INGREDIENTS

1 teaspoon olive oil
2 onions, finely diced
2 cloves garlic, crushed
500 g mixed mushrooms of your
 choice (e.g. shiitake, swiss or
 oyster), diced
1/2 cup white wine
1 teaspoon lemon juice
olive oil spray
85 g reduced-fat feta cheese,
 crumbled
3 tablespoons chopped fresh
 mixed herbs (e.g. sage, thyme,
 oregano, rosemary)
8 sheets filo pastry
freshly ground black pepper
broth
2 cups water
1 cup dried mushrooms
2 tablespoons tomato paste
1 tablespoon fresh herbs, chopped
 (e.g. parsley, basil, chives or
 coriander)
1 tablespoon sherry
**makes 2 strudels – each cuts into
 4 thick slices**

1 Heat the oil in a frying pan over a low heat. Add the onions and garlic. Cook, stirring, for 2–3 minutes or until soft and translucent. Add the mushrooms. Cook, stirring occasionally, for 5–8 minutes or until juices evaporate. Stir in the wine and lemon juice. Cook, stirring occasionally, until liquid is absorbed. Cool.

2 Preheat the oven to 180°C. Lightly spray or brush a baking tray with olive oil or line with nonstick baking paper. Set aside.

3 Stir the cheese and fresh herbs into mushroom mixture. Lay 2 sheets of filo pastry on a clean, dry work surface. Lightly spray or brush with olive oil and season with pepper. Place 2 more sheets on top. Place half the mushroom mixture along the long edge, leaving a 3 cm border at each end. Fold in the ends. Roll up tightly. Place strudel seam down on prepared baking tray. Repeat with remaining filo and mushroom mixture to make a second strudel. Using a sharp knife, make slashes in the top of each strudel to mark slices. Bake for 10–12 minutes or until golden.

4 To make the broth, place the water in a saucepan and bring to a boil. Add mushrooms, tomato paste, herbs and sherry. Boil until the mushrooms are tender and the mixture starts to thicken.

5 Cut the strudel where marked. Serve with or without the broth.

PREPARATION TIME
25 minutes

COOKING TIME
30–35 minutes

NUTRITIONAL VALUE PER SERVE	FAT 2.7 G	CARBOHYDRATE 13 G	PROTEIN 7.5 G

Salmon and potato bake

INGREDIENTS

1 teaspoon olive oil
1 onion, diced
2 stalks celery, diced
1 tablespoon tomato paste
225 g canned red or pink salmon,
  rinsed and drained
1 tablespoon chopped fresh tarragon
1⅕ cups low-fat milk
3 eggs, lightly beaten
2 egg whites, lightly beaten
juice of ½ lemon
freshly ground black pepper
4 large potatoes, thinly sliced
4 cups firmly packed spinach,
  blanched and squeezed of moisture
breadcrumb and parmesan topping
½ cup (stale bread) breadcrumbs
2 tablespoons fresh parsley, chopped
1 tablespoon parmesan cheese, grated
serves 4

1 To make the topping, place the breadcrumbs, parsley and cheese in a small bowl. Mix together and set aside.

2 Preheat the oven to 180°C. Lightly spray or brush a large flat casserole dish with oil.

3 Heat the oil in a nonstick frying pan over a medium heat. Add the onion and celery. Cook, stirring, for 3–4 minutes or until soft. Stir in the tomato paste. Cook for 3–4 minutes or until it becomes deep red and develops a rich aroma. Transfer the mixture to a large bowl. Cool.

4 Add the salmon, tarragon, milk, eggs, egg whites, lemon juice and pepper to taste to the onion mixture, and combine. Arrange half the potatoes over the base of the prepared dish. Pour over the salmon mixture. Top with the spinach. Cover with the remaining potatoes. Sprinkle with the topping. Bake for 1 hour or until the potatoes are tender and the mixture is set.

PREPARATION TIME
40 minutes

COOKING TIME
60–75 minutes

NUTRITIONAL VALUE PER SERVE	FAT 10 G	CARBOHYDRATE 32 G	PROTEIN 28.5 G

Tomato and chorizo muffins

INGREDIENTS

2 cups plain flour
4 teaspoons baking powder
¹⁄₂ teaspoon salt
1 egg
2 tablespoons olive oil
2 chorizo sausages
1¹⁄₄ cups milk
4 cherry tomatoes
parmesan cheese, shaved
makes 8

1 Preheat the oven to 190°C. Sift flour, baking powder and salt into a bowl. Make a well in the centre of the dry ingredients. Lightly beat egg and oil together until combined.

2 Cut sausages into 1 cm thick pieces. Mix sausages, egg mixture and milk into dry ingredients until just combined.

3 Fill greased deep muffin pans with mixture. Cut tomatoes in half crosswise. Place half a tomato on top of mixture, cut-side up.

4 Bake for 15 minutes or until muffins are cooked. Remove from oven and place a thin shaving of parmesan cheese over the top of each muffin.

PREPARATION TIME
10 minutes

COOKING TIME
15 minutes

NUTRITIONAL VALUE PER SERVE   FAT **13** G   CARBOHYDRATE **28** G   PROTEIN **10** G

Roasted capsicum muffins

INGREDIENTS

2 medium red capsicums
2 cups plain flour
4 teaspoons baking powder
$^1/_2$ teaspoon salt
1 egg
2 tablespoons olive oil
1 teaspoon chilli flakes
1 cup milk
makes 8

PREPARATION TIME
20 minutes

COOKING TIME
15 minutes

1 Preheat the oven to 190°C. Cut capsicums in half. Remove seeds and core and place cut side down on a baking tray. Grill until skins are blackened and blistered.

2 Transfer the capsicums into a plastic bag and allow to steam. When cool enough to handle, open the bag and slip the skins off the capsicum pieces. Cut capsicum halves in half again. Use a capsicum quarter to partly line the base and sides of greased deep muffin pans.

3 Sift flour, baking powder and salt into a bowl. Make a well in the centre of the dry ingredients. Lightly beat egg, oil and chilli together. Pour into dry ingredients with milk and mix quickly until just combined. Spoon mixture into capsicum-lined muffin pans to three-quarters full. Bake for 15 minutes. Serve upside down, split and filled with chilli jam or red capsicum relish.

NUTRITIONAL VALUE PER SERVE	FAT 7 G	CARBOHYDRATE 28 G	PROTEIN 6 G

Moroccan muffins

INGREDIENTS

1 cup couscous
1 cup boiling water
1 onion
2 tablespoons oil
2 teaspoons ground cumin
2 teaspoons ground coriander
1½ cups plain flour
4 teaspoons baking powder
½ teaspoon salt
2 eggs
1½ cups milk
½ cup raisins
makes 14

PREPARATION TIME
12 minutes

COOKING TIME
20 minutes

1 Preheat the oven to 190°C. Place couscous in a bowl. Pour over boiling water and set aside.

2 Peel onion and chop finely. Heat oil in a frying pan and cook onion for 5 minutes. Add cumin and coriander, and cook over a low heat until spices smell fragrant.

3 Sift flour, baking powder and salt into a bowl. Make a well in the centre of the dry ingredients. Lightly beat eggs. Add eggs, milk, raisins and onion mixture to dry ingredients and mix quickly until just combined.

4 Fill greased deep muffin pans with mixture. Bake for 15–20 minutes or until muffins spring back when lightly touched. Serve warm.

NUTRITIONAL VALUE PER SERVE   FAT 4.5 G   CARBOHYDRATE 22 G   PROTEIN 4.5 G

Prune and orange muffins

INGREDIENTS

1½ cups prunes, chopped
¼ cup brown sugar
1 cup orange juice
50 g butter
2 eggs
2 cups plain flour
3 teaspoons baking powder
makes 10

PREPARATION TIME
8 minutes

COOKING TIME
15 minutes

1 Preheat the oven to 190°C. Place prunes, brown sugar, orange juice and butter in a saucepan large enough to mix all the ingredients. Heat gently until butter melts. Remove from heat and cool.

2 Beat eggs into prune mixture with a wooden spoon. Sift in flour and baking powder and mix until just combined.

3 Three-quarters fill greased deep muffin pans with mixture.

4 Bake for 15 minutes or until muffins spring back when lightly touched.

NUTRITIONAL VALUE PER SERVE	FAT 5.5 G	CARBOHYDRATE 46 G	PROTEIN 5.5 G

Chocolate brownie muffins with mixed berry sauce

INGREDIENTS

250 g butter
$^1/_2$ cup cocoa
100 g dark chocolate
$1^1/_4$ cups sugar
4 eggs
2 teaspoons vanilla extract
$1^1/_4$ cups plain flour
1 teaspoon baking powder
mixed berry sauce
1 cup frozen mixed berries
$^1/_2$ cup mixed berry jam
$^1/_2$ cup ready-made chocolate sauce
makes 10

PREPARATION TIME
12 minutes

COOKING TIME
12 minutes

1 Preheat the oven to 180°C. Place butter, cocoa and chocolate in a saucepan large enough to mix all the ingredients. Melt over a medium heat. Stir in sugar and allow to cool.

2 Beat in eggs and vanilla extract. Sift over flour and baking powder and combine well.

3 Three-quarters fill greased muffin pans with mixture. Bake for 12 minutes.

4 To make the sauce, thaw berries and mash lightly. Place in a saucepan with jam. Heat until jam melts and berries are hot. Remove from heat and stir in chocolate sauce. Serve muffins warm with warm berry sauce and cream.

NUTRITIONAL VALUE PER SERVE	FAT 29 G	CARBOHYDRATE 68 G	PROTEIN 7.5 G

Bran and sticky raisin muffins

INGREDIENTS

1 cup wholemeal flour
1 teaspoon baking powder
$\frac{1}{2}$ teaspoon salt
1$\frac{1}{2}$ cups baking bran
$\frac{1}{4}$ cup sugar
1 cup raisins
50 g butter
2 tablespoons golden syrup
1$\frac{1}{4}$ cups milk
1 teaspoon bicarbonate of soda
1 egg, lightly beaten
makes 12

PREPARATION TIME
10 minutes

COOKING TIME
15 minutes

1 Preheat the oven to 200°C. Mix flour, baking powder, salt, bran, sugar and raisins together in a bowl. Make a well in the centre of the dry ingredients.

2 Melt butter and golden syrup together. Mix milk and bicarbonate of soda together. Pour butter mixture, milk and egg into dry ingredients and mix until just combined.

3 Three-quarters fill greased deep muffin pans with mixture. Bake for 10–15 minutes or until muffins spring back when lightly touched.

NUTRITIONAL VALUE PER SERVE	FAT 6.5 G	CARBOHYDRATE 35 G	PROTEIN 6 G

Apple strudel pudding

INGREDIENTS

560 g canned apple pieces
$^1/_2$ cup sultanas
$^1/_2$ teaspoon cinnamon powder
$^1/_2$ teaspoon ground nutmeg
1$^1/_2$ cups plain flour
2 teaspoons baking powder
$^3/_4$ cup rolled oats
2 eggs
$^1/_2$ cup brown sugar
50 g butter
1 cup milk
$^1/_2$ cup chopped pecans
serves 4–6

PREPARATION TIME
8 minutes

COOKING TIME
35 minutes

1 Preheat the oven to 190°C. Place apples, sultanas and spices in a medium sized mixing bowl and stir to combine.

2 Sift flour and baking powder into another bowl. Mix in oats. Make a well in the centre of the dry ingredients. Lightly beat eggs and sugar together until combined.

3 Melt butter. Mix egg mixture, butter and milk into dry ingredients until just combined.

4 Turn spiced apple mixture into a medium size baking dish. Pour flour mixture over apples, spreading to cover. Sprinkle with pecans. Bake for 30–35 minutes or until topping springs back when lightly touched. Serve hot with cream or ice cream.

NUTRITIONAL VALUE PER SERVE   FAT 23 G   CARBOHYDRATE 84 G   PROTEIN 12.5 G

Lemon and cinnamon eve's pudding

INGREDIENTS

500 g cooking apples, peeled, cored
  and chopped
100 g caster sugar
1 tablespoon water
$\frac{1}{2}$ teaspoon ground cinnamon
100 g butter, softened
finely grated zest of 1 lemon and
  juice of $\frac{1}{2}$ lemon
2 medium eggs, lightly beaten
100 g plain flour
$\frac{1}{2}$ teaspoon baking powder
serves 4

1 Preheat the oven to 180°C. Place the apples in a saucepan with 2 tablespoons of the sugar and the water. Cover and cook over a low heat for 3–4 minutes, until the apples begin to soften, then add the cinnamon and stir. Transfer to a 23 x 15 cm ovenproof dish.

2 Beat the butter and the remaining sugar until pale and creamy, then add the lemon zest and juice and the eggs. Sift in the flour and baking powder. Beat the mixture to a soft, dropping consistency.

3 Spoon the mixture over the apples, smooth with the back of a spoon, and bake for 25–30 minutes, until well risen, golden and just firm to the touch.

PREPARATION TIME
20 minutes

COOKING TIME
35 minutes

NUTRITIONAL VALUE PER SERVE	FAT 23 G	CARBOHYDRATE 57 G	PROTEIN 6.5 G

Date puddings with sticky toffee sauce

INGREDIENTS

100 g pitted dates, chopped
75 g butter, softened, plus extra for
   greasing
100 g soft light brown sugar
$\frac{1}{2}$ teaspoon vanilla extract
2 large eggs
100 g wholemeal flour
$1\frac{1}{2}$ teaspoons baking powder
1 very ripe banana, mashed
toffee sauce
85 g soft dark brown sugar
55 g butter
2 tablespoons light cream
serves 4

1 Preheat the oven to 180°C. Cover the dates with boiling water and soak for 10 minutes to soften.

2 Beat the butter, sugar and vanilla extract until pale and creamy. Beat in the eggs, then fold in the flour and baking powder. Strain the dates and blend to a purée in a food processor. Then stir into the mixture with the banana.

3 Spoon the mixture into four 200 ml greased pudding basins or ramekins, almost to their tops, and place on a baking sheet. Bake for 20 minutes until risen and just firm to the touch. Cool for 5 minutes, then loosen the puddings with a knife and invert onto plates.

4 To make the sauce, place the sugar, butter and cream in a pan and heat gently for 5 minutes or until syrupy. Pour over the puddings to serve.

PREPARATION TIME
20 minutes, plus
10 minutes soaking
and 5 minutes
cooling

COOKING TIME
25 minutes

| NUTRITIONAL VALUE PER SERVE | FAT 32.5 G | CARBOHYDRATE 83 G | PROTEIN 8.5 G |

Honey and almond friands

INGREDIENTS

100 g butter
¼ cup honey
4 egg whites
1 cup plain flour
½ cup icing sugar
topping
25 g butter
¼ cup honey
70 g slivered almonds
makes 6

PREPARATION TIME
10 minutes

COOKING TIME
20 minutes

1 Preheat the oven to 180°C. Melt butter and honey in a saucepan, heating until it starts to bubble. Remove from heat. Beat egg whites until lightly frothy in a bowl large enough to mix all the ingredients.

2 Sift flour and icing sugar into egg whites. Add butter mixture and fold in until flour and butter mixtures are combined with egg whites. Three-quarters fill greased friand or deep muffin pans with mixture.

3 To make the topping, melt butter, honey and almonds in a saucepan until boiling. Remove from heat and spoon over friands. Bake friands for 15–20 minutes or until cakes spring back when lightly touched.

NUTRITIONAL VALUE PER SERVE   FAT 24 G   CARBOHYDRATE 54 G   PROTEIN 7.5 G

Strawberry and cream tartlets

INGREDIENTS

145 g plain flour
1 tablespoon caster sugar
100 g unsalted butter, softened
finely grated zest of 1 small lemon,
    plus 1 teaspoon juice
145 ml double or whipping cream
250 g strawberries, halved
4 tablespoons raspberry jam or
    redcurrant jam to glaze
1 tablespoon water
1 tablespoon icing sugar, to dust
serves 4

PREPARATION TIME
25 minutes, plus
15 minutes chilling and
15 minutes cooling

COOKING TIME
20 minutes

1 Preheat the oven to 190°C. Sift the flour and sugar into a bowl.
   Rub in the butter and the lemon juice and knead lightly until
   the mixture forms a smooth dough. Cover with plastic wrap
   and refrigerate for 15 minutes.

2 Roll the dough out thinly on a lightly floured work surface,
   divide it into 4 and use it to line four 7½ cm greased, loose-
   bottomed tartlet tins. Line with baking paper and baking beans
   and bake for 15 minutes. Remove the paper and beans and cook
   for another 3–5 minutes until the pastry is golden. Leave to cool
   for 15 minutes, then remove from the tins.

3 Whip the cream with the lemon zest until it forms soft peaks.
   Spoon into the pastry cases and top with the strawberries. Melt
   the jam over a gentle heat with water, then press through a sieve
   and cool slightly. Spoon over the strawberries, then dust with
   icing sugar.

NUTRITIONAL VALUE PER SERVE	FAT 37 G	CARBOHYDRATE 51 G	PROTEIN 6 G

Banana filo tart

INGREDIENTS

8 sheets filo pastry
55 g unsalted butter, melted
3 large bananas, sliced
4 dried figs, sliced
30 g caster sugar
pinch of ground allspice
grated zest of 1 lemon
1 tablespoon dark rum
serves 4

PREPARATION TIME
20 minutes

COOKING TIME
15 minutes

1　Preheat the oven to 200°C. Place a baking tray on the top shelf to heat.

2　Brush a sheet of filo pastry with butter. Top with a second sheet and brush it with butter. Repeat with the remaining sheets until all the pastry has been used, then transfer to a cold baking tray.

3　Arrange the banana and fig slices over the pastry sheets, then scatter over the caster sugar, allspice and lemon zest. Pour the rum and any remaining butter over. Carefully transfer the tart to the heated baking tray and bake for 15 minutes or until golden and bubbling.

NUTRITIONAL VALUE PER SERVE　　　FAT **12** G　　　CARBOHYDRATE **47** G　　　PROTEIN **4.5** G

Apple tart easy

INGREDIENTS

250 g plain flour
125 g butter, cubed
2 tablespoons apricot jam
500 g cooking apples, peeled, cored
   and thinly sliced
1 teaspoon ground cinnamon
½ teaspoon allspice
finely grated zest of 1 orange
55 g soft light brown sugar
55 g sultanas
icing sugar to dust
serves 4

1 Preheat the oven to 190°C. Put the flour into a bowl and rub in the butter until the mixture resembles fine breadcrumbs. Add enough cold water (about 3–4 tablespoons) to make a smooth dough. Knead very lightly.

2 Roll out the pastry to a 35 cm round on a lightly floured work surface. Place on a large baking tray. Spread the jam over the centre of the pastry.

3 In a bowl, toss together the apples, cinnamon, allspice, orange zest, sugar and sultanas, then pile the mixture into the middle of the pastry. Bring the edges of the pastry up over the apple mixture, pressing into rough pleats leaving the centre of the pie open.

4 Bake for 35–45 minutes, until the pastry is golden, covering the pie with foil if the apple starts to burn. Sprinkle over the icing sugar before serving.

PREPARATION TIME
25 minutes

COOKING TIME
45 minutes

NUTRITIONAL VALUE PER SERVE	FAT 26.5 G	CARBOHYDRATE 91 G	PROTEIN 8 G

Individual chocolate apple cakes

INGREDIENTS

150 g butter
3/4 cup sugar
3 eggs
2 cups plain flour
1/4 cup cocoa
3 teaspoons baking powder
560 g canned apple slices
icing sugar to dust
makes 8

1 Preheat the oven to 180°C. Melt butter in a saucepan large enough to mix all the ingredients. Remove from heat and mix in sugar and eggs until combined.

2 Sift flour, cocoa and baking powder into mixture. Beat with a wooden spoon until smooth.

3 Half fill eight 6 x 5 cm paper cases with mixture. Top with apple slices then with chocolate mixture to fill the cases.

4 Bake for 15–20 minutes or until firm and cooked. Dust with icing sugar to serve.

PREPARATION TIME
10 minutes

COOKING TIME
20 minutes

| NUTRITIONAL VALUE PER SERVE | FAT 18.5 G | CARBOHYDRATE 54 G | PROTEIN 7.5 G |

Blueberry and orange clafoutis

INGREDIENTS

butter for greasing
200 g blueberries
3 medium eggs
75 g caster sugar
few drops vanilla extract
finely grated zest and juice
    of ½ orange
55 g plain flour, sifted
145 g sour cream
2 tablespoons butter, melted
icing sugar to dust
serves 4

PREPARATION TIME
10 minutes, plus
5 minutes cooling

COOKING TIME
40 minutes

1 Preheat the oven to 190°C. Grease a shallow 20 cm ovenproof dish
   with butter, then spoon in the blueberries.

2 Place the eggs, caster sugar, vanilla extract, orange zest and juice
   and the flour in a bowl, then beat until smooth. Gently stir in the
   sour cream and melted butter, then pour the mixture over the
   blueberries.

3 Bake for 40 minutes or until risen and set. Cool for 5 minutes, then
   dust with icing sugar.

NUTRITIONAL VALUE PER SERVE	FAT 27 G	CARBOHYDRATE 37 G	PROTEIN 8.5 G

Austrian maple spice cake

INGREDIENTS

3 cups plain flour
3 teaspoons baking powder
2 tablespoons cinnamon
1 teaspoon ground cloves
2 teaspoons ground ginger
2 tablespoons cocoa
1 cup maple syrup
$\frac{1}{2}$ cup of honey, warmed
1$\frac{1}{2}$ cups caster sugar
1$\frac{1}{2}$ cups of buttermilk
1 teaspoon vanilla extract
glaze
200 g dark cooking chocolate
2 tablespoons butter
juice and zest of 1 small orange
3 tablespoons marmalade or apricot jam
4 tablespoons sugar
2 teaspoons water
100 g milk chocolate, grated
serves 12

PREPARATION TIME
10 minutes, plus
5 minutes cooling

COOKING TIME
1 hour 15 minutes

1 Butter a nonstick 28 cm or 26 cm springform tin and set aside. Preheat the oven to 170°C.

2 In a large bowl, mix together the flour, baking powder, cinnamon, ground cloves, ginger and cocoa. In a separate bowl, whisk the maple syrup, honey, caster sugar, buttermilk and vanilla extract. Gently but thoroughly combine the flour mixture and the syrup mixture.

3 Pour the batter into the prepared cake tin and bake for 1 hour and 10 minutes. Remove from the oven and cool thoroughly.

4 When the cake is cold, remove from the cake tin. Warm the marmalade or jam and gently spread it over the surface of the cake. Allow to cool.

5 To make the glaze, melt the chocolate and butter, in the microwave. When melted, whisk in the orange juice thoroughly.

6 When the chocolate mixture is smooth, pour it over the marmalade-topped cake and spread it to cover.

8 Cut the zest of the orange into long fine strips. Heat the sugar and water together in a small saucepan, add the zest and simmer for 5 minutes. Lift out the caramelised zest and allow to cool. Discard the syrup.

9 Before serving, pile the grated chocolate and caramelised orange zest in the centre of the cake.

NUTRITIONAL VALUE PER SERVE	FAT 9 G	CARBOHYDRATE 105 G	PROTEIN 6 G

Very lemon cakes

INGREDIENTS

150 g softened butter
$\frac{1}{2}$ cup sugar
1 cup lemon curd
1 teaspoon lemon zest
3 eggs, beaten
1 cup plain flour
3 teaspoons baking powder
$\frac{1}{2}$ cup custard powder
$\frac{1}{2}$ cup sugar cubes
$\frac{1}{4}$ cup lemon juice
makes 6

PREPARATION TIME
10 minutes, plus
10 minutes cooling

COOKING TIME
40 minutes

1 Preheat the oven to 180°C. Beat butter, sugar, lemon curd and lemon zest together with a wooden spoon until combined.

2 Mix eggs into butter mixture. Sift in flour, baking powder and custard powder and combine. Half fill greased jumbo muffin pans or fancy cake tins with the mixture. Lightly crush sugar cubes and sprinkle over cakes.

3 Bake for 30–35 minutes or until cakes spring back when lightly touched. Pour lemon juice over cakes and bake a further 5 minutes.

4 Cool in tin for 10 minutes before removing.

NUTRITIONAL VALUE PER SERVE	FAT 35.5 G	CARBOHYDRATE 78 G	PROTEIN 9 G

Chocolate-mocha cake

INGREDIENTS

185 g dark chocolate, broken into
    small pieces
4 eggs, separated
1/2 cup caster sugar
185 g unsalted butter, softened and
    cut into pieces
2 tablespoons strong black coffee
1/2 cup plain flour
chocolate glaze
200 g dark chocolate, broken into
    small pieces
100 g unsalted butter
2 tablespoons water
serves 8

PREPARATION TIME
30 minutes

COOKING TIME
30 minutes, plus
2 hours refrigeration

1 Place chocolate in a bowl resting over a saucepan of simmering water for 5 minutes, or
   until chocolate melts. Remove from heat and stir until smooth. Set aside to cool.

2 Preheat the oven to 160°C. Place egg yolks and caster sugar in a bowl and beat until pale
   and fluffy. Add butter and beat egg mixture until creamy. Add coffee and chocolate and
   continue beating mixture until creamy. Sift flour over mixture and fold in lightly.

3 Beat egg whites until soft peaks form. Lightly fold into chocolate mixture. Pour into a
   greased and lined 20 cm round cake tin and bake for 30 minutes or until firm to touch.
   Turn off oven and cool cake in oven with door ajar. Remove from tin and refrigerate for 2
   hours or overnight.

4 To make the glaze, melt the chocolate and butter in a bowl resting over a saucepan of
   simmering water. Remove from heat and stir ingredients to combine. Set aside to cool.

5 Remove cake from refrigerator and place on a wire rack. Place on a tray and pour glaze
   over cake, smoothing it over the edges and onto the sides with a spatula. Leave until
   completely set. Transfer cake to a flat serving platter and cut into slices to serve.

NUTRITIONAL VALUE PER SERVE	FAT 47.5 G	CARBOHYDRATE 47 G	PROTEIN 7 G

Glossary

Al dente: Italian term to describe pasta and rice that are cooked until tender but still firm to the bite.

Asafoetida: a herbaceous perennial plant native to Iran. The dried sap is used as a spice. It resembles onion and garlic in flavour.

Bake blind: to bake pastry cases without their fillings. Line the raw pastry case with greaseproof paper and fill with raw rice or dried beans to prevent collapsed sides and puffed base. Remove paper and fill 5 minutes before completion of cooking time.

Baste: to spoon hot cooking liquid over food at intervals during cooking to moisten and flavour it.

Beat: to make a mixture smooth with rapid and regular motions using a spatula, wire whisk or electric mixer; to make a mixture light and smooth by enclosing air.

Beurre manié: equal quantities of butter and flour mixed together to a smooth paste and stirred bit by bit into a soup, stew or sauce while on the heat to thicken. Stop adding when desired thickness results.

Bind: to add egg or a thick sauce to hold ingredients together when cooked.

Blanch: to plunge some foods into boiling water for less than a minute and immediately plunge into iced water. This is to brighten the colour of some vegetables; to remove skin from tomatoes and nuts.

Blend: to mix 2 or more ingredients thoroughly together; do not confuse with blending in an electric blender.

Boil: to cook in a liquid brought to boiling point and kept there.

Boiling point: when bubbles rise continually and break over the entire surface of the liquid, reaching a temperature of 100°C (212°F). In some cases food is held at this high temperature for a few seconds then heat is turned to low for slower cooking. See simmer.

Bouquet garni: a bundle of several herbs tied together with string for easy removal, placed into pots of stock, soups and stews for flavour. A few sprigs of fresh thyme, parsley and bay leaf are used. Can be purchased in sachet form for convenience.

Caramelise: to heat sugar in a heavy-based pan until it liquefies and develops a caramel colour. Vegetables such as blanched carrots and sautéed onions may be sprinkled with sugar and caramelised.

Chill: to place in the refrigerator or stir over ice until cold.

Clarify: to make a liquid clear by removing sediments and impurities. To melt fat and remove any sediment.

Coat: to dust or roll food items in flour to cover the surface before the food is cooked. Also, to coat in flour, egg and breadcrumbs.

Cool: to stand at room temperature until some or all heat is removed, e.g. cool a little, cool completely.

Cream: to make creamy and fluffy by working the mixture with the back of a wooden spoon, usually refers to creaming butter and sugar or margarine. May also be creamed with an electric mixer.

Croutons: small cubes of bread, toasted or fried, used as an addition to salads or as a garnish to soups and stews.

Crudite: raw vegetable sticks served with a dipping sauce.

Crumb: to coat foods in flour, egg and breadcrumbs to form a protective coating for foods which are fried. Also adds flavour, texture and enhances appearance.

Cube: to cut into small pieces with six even sides, e.g. cubes of meat.

Cut in: to combine fat and flour using 2 knives scissor fashion or with a pastry blender, to make pastry.

Deglaze: to dissolve dried out cooking juices left on the base and sides of a roasting dish or frying pan. Add a little water, wine or stock, scrape and stir over heat until dissolved. Resulting liquid is used to make a flavoursome gravy or added to a sauce or casserole.

Degrease: to skim fat from the surface of cooking liquids, e.g. stocks, soups, casseroles.

Dice: to cut into small cubes.

Dredge: to heavily coat with icing sugar, sugar, flour or cornflour.

Dressing: a mixture added to completed dishes to add moisture and flavour, e.g. salads, cooked vegetables.

Drizzle: to pour in a fine thread-like stream moving over a surface.

Egg wash: beaten egg with milk or water used to brush over pastry, bread dough or biscuits to give a sheen and golden brown colour.

Essence: a strong flavouring liquid, usually made by distillation. Only a few drops are needed to flavour.

Fillet: a piece of prime meat, fish or poultry which is boneless or has all bones removed.

Flake: to separate cooked fish into flakes, removing any bones and skin, using 2 forks.

Flame: to ignite warmed alcohol over food or to pour into a pan with food, ignite then serve.

Flute: to make decorative indentations around the pastry rim before baking.

Fold in: combining of a light, whisked or creamed mixture with other ingredients. Add a portion of the other ingredients at a time and mix using a gentle circular motion, over and under the mixture so that air will not be lost. Use a silver spoon or spatula.

Glaze: to brush or coat food with a liquid that will give the finished product a glossy appearance, and on baked products, a golden brown colour.

Grease: to rub the surface of a metal or heatproof dish with oil or fat, to prevent the food from sticking.

Herbed butter: softened butter mixed with finely chopped fresh herbs and re-chilled. Used to serve on grilled meats and fish.

Hors d'oeuvre: small savoury foods served as an appetiser, popularly known today as 'finger food'.

Infuse: to steep foods in a liquid until the liquid absorbs their flavour.

Joint: to cut poultry and game into serving pieces by dividing at the joint.

Julienne: to cut some food, e.g. vegetables and processed meats, into fine strips the length of matchsticks. Used for inclusion in salads or as a garnish to cooked dishes.

Knead: to work a yeast dough in a pressing, stretching and folding motion with the heel of the hand until smooth and elastic to develop the gluten strands. Non-yeast doughs should be lightly and quickly handled as gluten development is not desired.

Line: to cover the inside of a baking tin with paper for the easy removal of the cooked product from the baking tin.

Macerate: to stand fruit in a syrup, liqueur or spirit to give added flavour.

Marinade: a flavoured liquid, into which food is placed for some time to give it flavour and to tenderise. Marinades include an acid ingredient such as vinegar or wine, oil and seasonings.

Mask: to evenly cover cooked food portions with a sauce, mayonnaise or savoury jelly.

Pan-fry: to fry foods in a small amount of fat or oil, sufficient to coat the base of the pan.

Parboil: to boil until partially cooked. The food is then finished by some other method.

Pare: to peel the skin from vegetables and fruit. Peel is the popular term but pare is the name given to the knife used; paring knife.

Pit: to remove stones or seeds from olives, cherries, dates.

Pith: the white lining between the rind and flesh of oranges, grapefruit and lemons.

Pitted: the olives, cherries, dates etc. with the stone removed, e.g. purchase pitted dates.

Poach: to simmer gently in enough hot liquid to almost cover the food so shape will be retained.

Pound: to flatten meats with a meat mallet; to reduce to a paste or small particles with a mortar and pestle.

Simmer: to cook in liquid just below boiling point at about 96°C (205°F) with small bubbles rising gently to the surface.

Skim: to remove fat or froth from the surface of simmering food.

Stock: the liquid produced when meat, poultry, fish or vegetables have been simmered in water to extract the flavour. Used as a base for soups, sauces, casseroles etc. Convenience stock products are available.

Sweat: to cook sliced onions or vegetables, in a small amount of butter in a covered pan over low heat, to soften them and release flavour without colouring.

Conversions

Measurements differ from country to country, so it's important to understand what the differences are. This Measurements Guide gives you simple 'at-a-glance' information for using the recipes in this book, wherever you may be.

Cooking is not an exact science – minor variations in measurements won't make a difference to your cooking.

EQUIPMENT

There is a difference in the size of measuring cups used internationally, but the difference is minimal (only 2–3 teaspoons). We use the Australian standard metric measurements in our recipes:

1 teaspoon ....5 ml   1 tablespoon....20 ml
1/2 cup......125 ml   1 cup.....250 ml
4 cups...1 litre

Measuring cups come in sets of one cup (250 ml), 1/2 cup (125 ml), 1/3 cup (80 ml) and 1/4 cup (60 ml). Use these for measuring liquids and certain dry ingredients.

Measuring spoons come in a set of four and should be used for measuring dry and liquid ingredients.

When using cup or spoon measures always make them level (unless the recipe indicates otherwise).

DRY VERSUS WET INGREDIENTS

While this system of measures is consistent for liquids, it's more difficult to quantify dry ingredients. For instance, one level cup equals: 200 g of brown sugar; 210 g of caster sugar; and 110 g of icing sugar.

When measuring dry ingredients such as flour, don't push the flour down or shake it into the cup. It is best just to spoon the flour in until it reaches the desired amount. When measuring liquids use a clear vessel indicating metric levels.

Always use medium eggs (55–60 g) when eggs are required in a recipe.

OVEN

Your oven should always be at the right temperature before placing the food in it to be cooked. Note that if your oven doesn't have a fan you may need to cook food for a little longer.

MICROWAVE

It is difficult to give an exact cooking time for microwave cooking. It is best to watch what you are cooking closely to monitor its progress.

STANDING TIME

Many foods continue to cook when you take them out of the oven or microwave. If a recipe states that the food needs to 'stand' after cooking, be sure not to overcook the dish.

CAN SIZES

The can sizes available in your supermarket or grocery store may not be the same as specified in the recipe. Don't worry if there is a small variation in size – it's unlikely to make a difference to the end result.

dry		liquids	
metric (grams)	imperial (ounces)	metric (millilitres)	imperial (fluid ounces)
		30 ml	1 fl oz
30 g	1 oz	60 ml	2 fl oz
60 g	2 oz	90 ml	3 fl oz
90 g	3 oz	100 ml	3 1/2 fl oz
100 g	3 1/2 oz	125 ml	4 fl oz
125 g	4 oz	150 ml	5 fl oz
150 g	5 oz	190 ml	6 fl oz
185 g	6 oz	250 ml	8 fl oz
200 g	7 oz	300 ml	10 fl oz
250 g	8 oz	500 ml	16 fl oz
280 g	9 oz	600 ml	20 fl oz (1 pint)*
315 g	10 oz	1000 ml (1 litre)	32 fl oz
330 g	11 oz		
370 g	12 oz		
400 g	13 oz		
440 g	14 oz		
470 g	15 oz		
500 g	16 oz (1 lb)		
750 g	24 oz (1 1/2 lb)		
1000 g (1 kg)	32 oz (2 lb)		*Note: an American pint is 16 fl oz.

cooking temperatures	°C (celsius)	°F (fahrenheit)	gas mark
very slow	120	250	1/2
slow	150	300	2
moderately slow	160	315	2–3
moderate	180	350	4
moderate hot	190	375	5
	200	400	6
hot	220	425	7
very hot	230	450	8
	240	475	9
	250	500	10

Index